Life's Challenges, Experiences And Blessings

By Marionette Simmons

Cover Design/Artwork by: Marionette Simmons

Design by: Marionette Simmons

Photography by: Marionette Simmons

Order this book online at www.trafford.com
or email orders@trafford.com

Most Trafford titles are also available at major online book retailers.

Printed in the United States of America.

ISBN: 978-1-4251-4064-9 (sc)

Trafford rev. 08/01/2013

www.trafford.com

North America & international
toll-free: 1 888 232 4444 (USA & Canada)
fax: 812 355 4082

Life's Challenges, Experiences And Blessings

A Collection of Poetry
By
Marionette Simmons

Dedications

To My Mom
She has been my inspiration at all times; in whatever I put my hands to she has supported me. I owe her much gratitude, love and thank her for always encouraging me to follow my dreams.

To My Sister
Marchelle, the other poet of the family, has also encouraged me and respected our similar aspiration. Thank you for also believing in me and pushing me to make this step a reality.

To My Beautiful Daughter
Kelly, you don't know this but I write this book for you. This is to show you that whatever you aspire to be or do in this life you can do. Don't let anything or anyone dash your dreams or expectations. Life is what you make it and I dedicate this book to you and say look, Mommy made it.

Introduction

Many years ago, during my high school days, I would sit and write poetry for fun and laughs. A friend of mine from school also wrote so we would share our ideas and styles. As time passed, it turned into an outlet for expressing suppressed feelings of emotion, which turned into a pure love to write and share.

Later, I found that writing was a hobby that allowed me to interact with people of similar interest or just share my writings with others who enjoyed reading poetry from a friend. My sister and I wrote and shared our poetry with one another and often spoke of publishing a book one day. Like many people who talk, we procrastinated for some time as we thought of many established authors and wondered could we really do it.

After writing for many years about family relations, love gone good or bad, sympathies for people who had lost love ones and many other things, I decided to start a yearly poem which I dedicated to Mothers. Of course with the support of my mother this was the best dedication I could have made to her each year. In the process of writing these poems I became a mother and received a new perspective and purpose to write poems dedicated to mothers.

In the first section of this book: "Tributes To Mothers", you will find poetry dedicated to mothers and I hope you enjoy them. My favorite being "A Tribute to all Mothers" that speaks to mothers who did and did not give birth but plays a vital role of a mother.

The next section of this book: "Expressions" speaks to life's challenges. Some of them may relate to you and your everyday situations. My life-long friend "Arthur Robinson", the father of my child, has inspired many of them.

The third section of this book: "Family Time" is easy reading for the whole family of any age. Read it to your children or let them enjoy it for themselves.

The fourth and final section of this book: "Time For God" is dedicated to my daughter "Kelly Simmons". As we celebrate our relationship with God and enjoy His presence, so too I hope that you enjoy the writings in this section.

I believe in making the most of the gifts God gives on loan to us during our lifetime, therefore I share one of mine with you.

God's many blessing to the readers of this book.

Table Of Contents

Prayer of Thanks

Lord I'm thankful for the opportunity that has been afforded to me
To share this book with many and especially my family
My hope is that it brings them joy, peace and laughter as they read
Let some kind word written help them in life to heed
As it throws many a challenge their way
Teach them Lord to know, in "You" they can stay.

I'm thankful for the gifts that God has laid before me
I offer them back to "Him" in thanks
I count it a privilege that I can share with others
My talents, time and life's experiences
I am thankful not only to God but to those who have stood by me and supported my every endeavor, to them I owe a hearty thank you.

Lest we forget, all things come from thee, O Lord and therefore I acknowledge You, praise You, and give thanks unto You.

Amen.

Author: Marionette & daughter Kelly Simmons

Part One

"Dedications To Mothers"

A Mother's Wish, A Child's Response

Child my prayer is that you walk upright in the way you were taught
Mother, I have been taught well, but my will is strong
Child, let the strength of your will bring out the best in you and not the worst
Mother, there is so much peer pressure and influence out there
Child, do not give in and do not give up for these things are to test what has been instilled in you for such a time as this
Mother, thank you for the opportunity to talk about anything with you
Child, know that I am here to support you when you are right and let you know when you are wrong for your own good
Mother, help me to stand for what is right, to not be a follower, but a leader and let my will be guided by God
Child, let us pray, that what you do will be pleasing unto me, and God.

Comfort for the Grieving Mother

As I reflect over the last couple of years
I have seen the faces of many grieving mothers on our news
Grieving for their sons and daughters, that have passed from here to eternity
Some are grieving because of injustice from our judicial system
And some are grieving because of unanswered questions

Grieving mothers, may you find comfort this day
In the fact that the Lord is the way
He can heal your broken heart
And give you a brand new start

If the wound is open, this is hard to see
But the comforter is there for you if only you just believe

May the memories of your love ones comfort you this day
And may the joy of the Lord be your strength.

A Tribute to all Mothers

What is a Mother?

Is she the woman who brought you into this world?
Or is she that person who nurtured you from a little boy or girl

Is she the one who taught you right from wrong?
Or the one who sang you a lullaby song

Is she the one who taught you God's Word?
And led you on a right path regarding the bees and the birds

Is she the one who stayed up with you all night?
When you were sick she made sure everything was all right

Or is she that big sister or friend
Who loves you although she didn't put life into your limbs

You don't have to give birth to a child
To be a mother for a lifetime or for a little while
It's a role that many of us play
Which stabilizes someone's life today

So if you are a mother in the true sense of the word
Or one who has shared themselves without the need to be heard

My prayer and best wishes go out to you this day
In love and gratitude
"Happy Mother's Day"

The Characteristics of a Mother

A mother's touch, so soft and sweet
It's almost like a gentle breeze
A mother's hand so firm but loving
As she disciplines her seed

A mother's love unlike no other
Always felt, even if it's not expressed
A mother's heart always yearning
For her child to have the very best

A mother's ways, always caring
For her own and others too
A mother's home, she's always sharing
With family and neighbors too

A mother's laughter fills the air
Resembling an aroma of sweet perfume
Like a mother's joy with the birth of an heir
As it is brought forth from her womb.

The characteristics of a mother is often displayed
With many fine attributes and warm accolades
So children, embrace the character of your mother today
And Mothers continue to live as positive examples now and always.

To All The Mothers'

A mother is not just someone who gives birth,
She's someone who labors and shows her worth,
She's that person, who stayed up with you all through the night,
When you were sick or lonely she held you tight.

Sometimes a mother can be your best friend,
To laugh with, cry with, the list never ends,
It takes all kinds to make mothers today,
Some of us are close with them, and sometimes we both stray.

Remembering the days when mother's were at home,
Seems so far away almost unknown,
Times have changed so drastically, that sometimes we forget,
These were the best years to instill the values at best,
To these children that made us mothers today,
To give them a foundation, teach them not to stray.

This message is to the mother's of old,
Teach the young mother's of the fold,
How to be strong, wise and true,
Remembering some of the trials you've been through.

To the children, for we are truly blessed,
Cherish your mother always, no matter what you do,
God gave you to them at the time you were born,
Sometimes you made them proud, happy and even mourn.

Now it's time to reflect over the past
And bring forth laughter and joy that will last.

A Mother's Day Sentiment

At first there was a woman made from Adam's side
Whom God gave him to be fruitful and multiply
This was another new beginning of life and birth
Which mother's have been blessed with on this earth

God knew "man" could not endure this pain
So he gave it to a woman to bear and claim
Precious gifts came forth, that's what your children are
As you hear stories from mothers both near and far

It sometimes takes a nation to raise a child
A mother to bear or carry him for a while
And when that life is brought into this world
It changes you completely to hold this little boy or girl

Women, you are blessed to be mother's today
Teach a child in the way it should grow and they will never stray
Show them love and nurture them too
Set a solid foundation to carry them through

Children, make your mothers proud to call you their sons &
daughters
Show them in little ways that you love them and appreciate them
Even if it's a hug a day, kind words or a smile

Mothers enjoy your day as it comes by
May you feel the love of your family ties
God bless you all, is my prayer
As you spend time with those who you hold dear.

Published in "On the Wings of Poetry"
Edited by: Lavender Aurora

A Mother's Love

A mother's love is shown in how she cares
A mother's love is shown in how she shares
A mother's love is expressed when she stays by your side
Like the day she gave birth to you the tears she could not hide

When you are sick and shut in she is there for you
When you are in trouble most times she bails you out too
A mother will pray for her child when she has never prayed before
A mother will have her heart broken for the things her child can't endure

A mother's love will issue out the rod of correction
As she knows that this will lead you later in the right direction
A mother is a gift from God just like the child she is given
Woman came from Adam's rib but mothers were truly sent from heaven

Mother's I hope you are loved by your offspring not just today
But all the days of your lives
Remember that God loves and watches over you each and every day
Mother's be blessed today and always
Stay strong, find happiness and enjoy each day like it was your last.

Part Two

"Expressions"

Moments of Silence

Moments of silence I cherish each day
In the noisy environment with which I stay
Sometimes they are joyous noises of children that I adore
And other times it is simply chaos and uproar
Dealing with constant noises around me
Is not exactly my specialty
I love my peace and quiet in all respects
In these moments of silence I'm at my best
It's a time when things become so clear
Like a problem in a distance that remained a blur
A moment of serenity
A moment when you can let yourself be free.

Listen

Listen quietly as the voice of loneliness speaks
Caught between the four walls with drifting thoughts to seek
Trying to break loose from this non-existent lifestyle
Drifting almost permanently knowing it'll only last a while
Search deep inside yourself and find what you want out of life
Dreaming hopelessly of making a man you love his devoted wife
Knowing this should be a minor phase of time
You can't surrender this overwhelming thought that's running through your mind
Searching endlessly for something positive to hold on to
Something that is stable that can keep you busy and interested too
Try not to bury yourself in any form of love affair
You may wind up back in your lonely state totally unaware
Listen quietly as the voice of loneliness can finally chime
Now I've found something to consume me and occupy my time.

Toils of Life

Have you ever known a time of confusion
When the question you ask yourself has no solution
Or if someone else asks a question and you can't find the conclusion
Is this reality or just an illusion?
A baffling life is what I'm often leading
Making decisions that are sometimes misleading
Trying to please some of the people I meet
I should really stop and think about me
I have to ask myself what am I really looking for
Or am I looking at all
Although someone else is hoping and looking for more
That doesn't mean that I have to carry the ball
I'm usually left in an indecisive position
So all I do is watch, sit and listen
They wait for an answer and sometimes in demand
Decisions like this I cannot stand
It's usually a matter of choice
Trying to avoid hearing anyone's voice
Friendship in all I can offer at this time
Anything more intimate is out of my line
You can't please all of the people all of the time
So I guess you'll have to just accept my rhyme

Tragedies that Arise when Things look Good

Why must life treat me this way
You find love but is it really there to stay
When things are going oh so well
And one thing or another spoils what is going swell
It's almost as if happiness was not meant to be
With all the pain and suffering confronting me
Am I suppose to love at all
Must I always be the one to take the fall
Loving you is all I can ever think of
You tell me it's all over without a pause
I guess I'm suppose to accept whatever it is you say
I can't, since my love for you grows stronger each and every day
I'm not sure how much you relate to what I say
I'm not sure how deep your feelings are for me at this rate
You say: "substitute me for another man"
This is only a cop out, don't you understand
You cannot switch love off and on
Once it's in your heart all other thoughts are gone
You may think that there are others standing in line
Believe me I'm not about to waste my time
It's you I love and not another
So put your best foot forward and make this relationship last so we can be together.

Playing the Roll of Second Best

Many times people don't realize they are really playing the second best roll
Their partner or mate often has a good excuse to try and remain in control
They play with your emotions, they promise all sorts of things
While they engage the company of another as they pull your strings
The one who is playing this sick joke doesn't care if you get hurt
This doesn't faze them in the least; they're only going thru a spurt
They think they can play games with you like you have no mind of your own
Gain your own self-control even if it means being all alone
Sometimes this may cause you to feel depressed or devastated too
But instead find inner strength don't give up, there won't be anything you can't do
They always say there is someone for everyone in this life
If you plan on playing second best you know it can't be right
It should be something solid that only two can share
Then you can consider it a real and true love affair.

What Is Love

Love is: When you can "Share" someone's pain and help them through it
Love is: Holding onto what you have as a mean of "Security"
Love is: "Understanding" yourself and partner and knowing some of their limitations
Love is: "Trusting" someone without ever being doubtful of anything you hear about them which sounds convincing
Love is: "Caring" for an individual to an extent when you would do just about anything for them
Love is: "Sharing" your inner-most feelings with the right someone whose feelings are on a mutual level with yours
Love is: Being "Thoughtful" and considering each others moods, likes, dislikes and habits
Love is: Being so involved with someone that it can take you from reality to a land of "Dreaming"
Love is: Allowing yourself to become emotional and "Considering" each others "Emotions" and "Feelings"
Love is: An actual "Need" or urge not only for the individual's body, but also for their "Companionship" and "Friendship"
Love is: "Unity", thinking about things with the same intentions in mind but not necessarily reading the other's mind
Love is: "Fulfilling" a place of loneliness with yourself
Love is: Finding "Peace" within yourself to be "Tolerant" of others actions
Love is" "Helping" each other in times of need or to reach a goal and standing by them if they fail
Love is: "Togetherness" enjoying each others company as well as other people
These are the Consistencies of Love.

Fulfillment Found in God's Gift

Many times we look back over our lives and wonder
Where have I been and why was I there
We sometimes don't know, but God knows

He gives us time to mend from our brokenness
So that we can receive the gift He has for us
The fulfillment we know nothing about

He sends an angel just when we think
Is there someone for me Lord?
And He sends that someone to make us whole, for He did not mean for us to be alone

The Word of God in the book of "Ecclesiastes 3 …"
Speaks about times and purposes under heaven
The Word of God in the book of "Genesis 2…"
Tells about the two that shall become one

I thank God today, for the Fulfillment of His Gift

Omar
You are Maxine's Fulfillment
You are Her Destiny
You are Her Time to Dance
You are Her Time to Live
You are Her Time to Laugh

Maxine
You are Omar's Fulfillment
You are His Rose amongst the Thorns
You are His Queen
You are His Time to Embrace
You are His Time to Love

You are Each Other's Fulfillment of God's Gift

"Dedication to my sister, Maxine and her husband Omar on their Wedding Day, May 3, 2007"

Part Three

"Family Time"

The Postman in the Village

He is such a very pleasant man
Always willing to lend a hand
He helps out in anyway he can
He is truly a good and reliable postman
He helped me out on this sunny day
He even showed me how to reduce the postage I had to pay
He will be considered a true friend indeed
With his wide smile, consistency and his dash of speed
My thanks go out to him on this day
For he has made it a pleasant Tuesday

Children

As babies they are oh so sweet
Loving, tender and oh so meek
Though when they start to grow up
All the mischievous things they do never stops
They repeat everything they hear
These are the kinds of things you have to bear
This is also something that is quite often done
Despite the fact of where it comes from
This is only a very small part of their character in life
That helps to make them tough and bright
So don't try to calm them down
You'll never stop them; they'll keep on running around
Then the time will come for them to go to school
You try your best to prepare them to be calm and cool
You instill in them, this is their time to learn
A good education is what they will earn
So bring your children up in the right way
You will find that they will never stray
You will also find you have gained a helping hand
It is something you would be thankful for in the end.

You are my Brother and you are my Friend

I'm glad to know we share an unspoken bond
That cannot change with time
And I know you care deep down inside
Though expressing it all the time, is not who you are

You have a quiet spirit, gentle and subtle
It's the strength of your demeanor and your character
Your love for family has shown through the ages
Let us never take it for granted or that it comes and goes in stages

Sometimes we forget or just don't bother to tell someone we love them
Or even that we care
So this is a perfect time my brother to let you know
You are loved most dear

I call you my friend as you have stood beside me
And shared my pain and also comforted me
These are things we cherish and never forget
My brother I wish you all good things today
& God's many richest blessings.

Dedicated to my brother: Michael Simmons

Chemeca

Chemeca, my sweet and beautiful niece
Whenever she's mad and cries she never thinks to cease
I hope you will grow to be neat and kind
Never leave any loose ends behind
It seems you will grow to be a brilliant young lady
Don't let you thoughts become dull or shady
Try to make everything interesting to hear
So people will listen with an attentive ear
Watch your moves don't make them too soon
Eventually you may find that they're all doomed
If you are sure of what you are getting into
Then just go ahead and follow through.

The Dad I can proudly call my Father

You have been the greatest father to me
The dad I will treasure always you see
You have been there for me when I was feeling low
You are always there for Mom and the family and let us know
You've shown us love and sacrifice
We've all learned from you it was worth the fight
You poured out your love to children of your wife
You never complained for our entrance into your life
I'm truly proud to call you my father
You've been great unlike no other
So Daddy, as you celebrate this Father's Day
Remember I love you as if you were my natural father today.

The Trip Over

A very, very long trip indeed
With the pleasant company it was a dash of speed
I talked my head off from the time I got on the plane
With the friendly people all around I exclaim
The word search book quickly became a bore
And before I knew it I was in Baltimore
I talked with a guy with a possible job at home
I guess you really don't need a travel companion because I'm not alone
I saw a Bermudian guy I knew
I even tried to sit by him too
Unfortunately the plane was full to the gills
All my seatmates were far from being a pill
So far the trip has been an enjoyable one
I really hope I continue to have so much fun
The music had a lot to be desired
It didn't exactly thrill me or set my life on fire
Although it was better than what we were getting at home
A little rock and roll to let the old imagination roam
Well, I'm beginning to tire myself out right now
The trip is too long for boredom to be allowed
I guess this is my cue to bring this to an end
After all I am finally on land.

Cooper Ward

Denise was the first one I met
The nice Scottish girl of silhouette
She did something to me that took me back to my youth
My body has the proof; I tell you it's the truth
I don't hold it against her
It's just something that had to be
Then came Norma with her chipper smile
Making me feel comfortable all the while
Working hand in hand with Dar so near
Pampering me terribly and keeping the cheer
At this point things were getting a little frightful for me
Dr. Simmons was waiting in the operating room so patiently
They tried to assure me that all is well
The stay since then has really been swell
Then in the evening came Kelly, Linda and Sally
And I often heard the name in the corridor of a Mrs. Smellie
They were all so great I didn't believe this could be
Especially since it was all happening to me
I can't remember the names of everyone that has been so helpful and great in here
If I have forgotten you don't take it to heart I really care
Being on this ward has been the greatest experience for me
And the care I've received from all of you I wouldn't trade
So thank you all and God bless you too
As I am homeward bound after this time spent with you.

Hospital Life

Sometimes it is frightening, sometimes funny
It doesn't require brains or even money
Some of these people are really grand
Some of them off the wall and a little off hand
One morning I had a nurse she was really dizzy
She repeated herself constantly she was really silly
The staff seems to change so often each day
I'm glad to see there's a few faithful who stay
They've been the greatest of help to me
Especially for being in the hospital for the first time you see
It's been quite an experience here to say the least
Not something I'll trade for Mom's good home feast
All and all it's been bearable inside
In a few days they will give me the slide
Out the door and hopefully not to return a moment too soon
Just to visit and not to stay, truly this is good news.

Pay Attention

The mode is set, the classroom scene
No time for fooling around, no time to daydream
The lecturer speaks, pay attention it is for you
Are the instructions clear, do you know what to do
Set your goals, there is something to achieve
Not just good grades, but a sense of ease
Looking forward to the prize that awaits at the end
A college diploma, a career, a chance to make a stand
What a wonderful sense of accomplishment you'll feel
When you apply yourself to a college education, this can all be for real.

Part Four

"Time for God"

God's Love

The love of God is an unspeakable joy
When His son died, all our sins He destroyed
He died upon the cross of Calvary
So we may have everlasting life and peace
His guidance takes us through each and every day
Close by His side we will stay
As long as you are serving Him, you know He's by your side
Jesus is the solid rock, so there is never a reason to hide
Just as you are good and true
God's love will always be there for you
Remember without a shadow of a doubt
He will always bring you out
No matter how big a sin you may commit
He will forgive you, and He won't call it quits.

A Gift from God

People are often given gifts from God
And fail to use them for the right cause
A gift to paint, a gift to sing
It can be given in any form or thing
An inborn talent is a special gift
Which may one day give someone a spiritual lift
Like a voice softly singing a gospel song
To carry them through all day long
Talents are not the only kinds of gift given from God
The life of a loved one you thought you had lost
The joy of watching a life being born
Is the greatest gift that God had spawned

Humble Thyself unto the Lord

I often think to myself, what the true meaning of humility is
So I looked it up and this is the definition it gives
Self-abasement, submission, lack of pride and a lack of modesty
This in fact is a tall order for our human frailty

Then I remembered how the word of God so aptly, put it to us
We are in this world, but not of this world, so I stopped all the fuss
Knowing all of this, it was only easier said then done
Each day as we try to get pass the pride and the big one submit, is the battle really won

That's why the Word says: seek the Lord's face day by day
Study His Word diligently and always pray
Ask Him to help you to let go of the "old man" called self
And seek His will for your life, not yours or anybody else

Behold The Glory of the Lord

As I behold the glory of the Lord
My eyes see things they've never seen before
My ears are open in a way that appears strange but wonderful
My heart is receptive, and full of joy
As I behold the glory of the Lord.

The Psalmist says, this is the day that the Lord has made
Let us rejoice and be glad in it (Psalm 118:24)
When I think of God the Creator of heaven and earth
I can reflect on the fact that I was thought of, before I was conceived
He had a plan for my life before I called upon his name in faith
I can rejoice in his peace, forgiveness and everlasting love
As I behold the glory of the Lord

Romans12:2, says be transformed by the renewing of your mind that ye may
prove what is good, acceptable & perfect will of God,
Many times my mind thinks of something and my feet follow
If I am obedient to the will of God, then my actions will be acceptable
When I think of his goodness and all that he's done for me
My soul cries out hallelujah, praise God for saving me
As I behold the glory of the Lord

James 1:2-3, says my brethren: count it all joy when ye fall into divers temptations:
Knowing this, that the trying of your faith worketh patience
In the first month of my Christian experience, temptations seemed non-existent
Which gave me a chance to just grow and enjoy learning about the Lord
As the trials came I reflected on this passage and sought out patience with eagerness
Frustration and anger tried to keep a hold on me
As I prayed for an increase in faith to carry me through
God said he'll never leave you nor forsake you, which kept me in his grasp
For I knew as long as I hold fast to his Word these trials will surely pass
Praise him in the good times, and in the bad times, give him honor, glory and praise
Let the joy of the Lord be my strength, worship the Lord and praise his holy name
As I behold the glory of the Lord.

Thinking of God & Being in His Presence

Dear Lord teach me how to pray
As I learn to walk with you day by day
Show me the way you would have me to tread
As I explore this new life ahead
Each day as I learn more about you
I count it all joy, as the book of James tells me to
Teach me O Lord how to examine myself
To make sure I keep in the path of righteousness and not somewhere else
Give me a desire to feast on Your Word
Let it engulf me, overwhelm me like nothing I've ever heard
Bring me a step closer to you as I serve you each day
These are just a few things, Lord I pray
I reflect on a time of witnessing to someone who knows you not
They keep me on my toes, quite a lot
It's an experience I enjoy and a challenge too
Especially because it draws me closer to you
Use me Lord, as I try to obey your will and your way
Help me Lord to stay focused and not to stray
I know this spirit will often wrestle with this flesh
Thank God greater is He that is in me that can anoint me afresh
I'm thankful for the day that I answered your call
You brought me from darkness to light, in spite of it all
Help me to never take you for granted, my Creator, my God
For each day I have life, hope and a purpose for the road I trod

Fill me with your Holy Spirit all day and night
Let me ask what I can do for you, which is pleasing in your sight
Cleanse me that I may walk worthy of thee
Humble me to learn to pray always on bended knee
Lord you fill me with such joy that sometimes I can't explain
You are my strength in times of weakness and pain
My shepherd, my refuge, my high tower, my father
For in this world there is none other
Your "Word" says: thou shall have no other God's before me
It is difficult to deny self and selfishness to make room for thee
And yes I know, this is what I must do to totally make you Lord of my life
With my hand in yours and my faith in you, it will be all right.

A Woman of God

Oh woman of God, be thou encouraged by these words
They may be few, but they are from my heart
I have looked at you in my Christian life
I've even heard of some of your life's pain
I draw strength from you each time I encounter your presence
Which I cannot explain, but God knows

I look at you each week as you share a part of yourself
You share in your love of God in teaching His Word
You share your talents in the kitchen as we partake of your many delights
And so I take this opportunity to share something in return

I may not have the talent to cook a lovely meal
Or even to impart some words of wisdom
That's why God gave us you

God gave me other talents that I impart to you today
Words of expression that God gave me to say

He chose me as a vessel to sing His Holy Word
And chose you as a vessel to pray and teach His Holy Word
I'm thankful that we are part of his divine plan
I'm thankful that He has placed you in my midst.

I thank God for you
Be encouraged my sister.

My Secret Pal - A Woman of Wisdom

I found it quite amusing, the common things we share
Since I know you're a woman of wisdom with your words of care
I have been listening attentively as your sentiments were displayed
As cards were read, written by you, I stood in awe and amazed.
Wisdom of the old passed on to the youth is a precious gift to give
For as children of God we are taught to share & encourage as we live
You never know whose life you're touching from day to day
Or who you may be encouraging as you go on your merry way
It's like the way you light up the room when your favorite song is sung
"Come Let's Stroll down Blessed Boulevard" for you know the battle is won
The Psalmist says in (Psalm 92:1):
It is a good thing to give thanks unto the Lord and to sing praises unto thy name O most high
For we know that each day as we are given life we have something to thank God for
My prayer for you is to keep on pressing on the upward way
That God will strengthen you each and every day
That His hand will be upon you in your sitting and lying down
And you will always wear a smile and never a frown
For as long as we have the Lord on our side
We have hope to carry on and take each day in stride
Be encouraged my sister and my friend
Hold on everyday to God's unchanging hand
Love you in the precious Name of Jesus.

Acknowledgements

I would like to take this opportunity to thank some individuals who have helped make this dream a reality.

To my family who have always believed in me and encouraged me in whatever I have set my mind to do even when things may look bleak or out of my reach.

To my many co-workers who have encouraged me to publish my poetry in our local papers or as Ana would say, "Just go and write the book, I'll be the first to buy a copy". I intend to hold her to her word.

To the Bermuda College writers club who have allowed me the opportunity to publish my first pieces in our school's book.

To the International Library of Poetry who has afforded me the opportunity to publish my work in their anthology, they have been a great source of inspiration.

To On the Wings of Poetry for publishing my first official piece of work in their book, this was the stepping-stone to an open door.

To Sister Hattie who always acknowledges my writing ability as God's gift and never forgets to encourage me to press on and write what is in my heart and share it with others.

To my daughter who I will leave this to as a legacy of who her mother is and that nothing in life is impossible, if you act on your dreams that can become your fulfillments of tomorrow.

About the Author:

Marionette Simmons was born; raised and currently lives in Bermuda. One day, long ago, she thought that she was an average girl with ordinary dreams like any other girl her age. She started writing for fun during the latter part of her high school years and sang for kicks. As the years passed by, she continues to write, work, sing and above all enjoy motherhood with her little girl Kelly her one and only precious gem.

She has had opportunity to receive a few accolades from her writing such as a second place award for writing a tourism essay for her island home, Bermuda. Excitedly as she got her feet wet, she entered a series of her writings in her college's Writers Club competition during her studies at Bermuda College. She entered ten pieces and six were featured in their book. What an honor that was for her. They are also featured in this book for your pleasure: "Humble Thyself unto the Lord", "Thinking of God & Being in His Presence" to name a few. Other recognitions came yearly, as she composes a new Mother's Day tribute for many to enjoy.

She has dedicated many years to writing and has been inspired by many of life's experiences, expressions, travels and family. Having been encouraged by the many readers of her mother's day poems each year; Marionette decided to step out of her comfort zone and enter her poetry in a competition or two. She entered some of her writing into the International Library of Poetry and had the opportunity to be chosen for their Anthology and also The Whose Who of Poetry. She has also been chosen to feature one of her pieces with Famous Poets.com

Marionette also has one of her poems " Afraid to Love and Lose" featured in her sister, Marchelle Gibbons's recently published book of poetry "Cherished Moments".

Life's Challenges, Experiences and Blessings is a long life dream that has been kept on the back burner long enough and holds a collection of Marionette's work to be published. She looks at this challenge and blessing as a way to let her light shine, and let people know that life always has something new in store for you.

www.ingramcontent.com/pod-product-compliance
Ingram Content Group UK Ltd.
Pitfield, Milton Keynes, MK11 3LW, UK
UKHW041834200726
13854UKWH00003BA/1130

9 781425 140649